Weight!
I Am Trying to
Understand Life

Weight!
I Am Trying to
Understand Life

by

Linda Grebe Williams

DORRANCE PUBLISHING CO., INC.
PITTSBURGH, PENNSYLVANIA 15222

Dedication

My life has been blessed with some outstanding people who have supported me through both the good and the bad times, and I dedicate this book to them.

To my mother, Elizabeth Grebe, and my brothers, Bill and Richard Grebe, who have always been there for me for as long as I can remember.

To my sister, Sandy Kolonich, who has been a good friend these past few years and who has always been there to listen. (I have the phone bill to prove it!)

To my niece, Barbi Kolonich, who brings laughter and fun to my life.

To my friend, Charise Simpson. I found out what friendship was all about the day we became friends.

To my friend, Michael Droll. I thank him for believing in me and for teaching me to believe in myself. It's a gift I could never repay.

To my children, Joshua, Ashley, and Jon. They teach me about life every day. I am very proud of each of them, and I love them.

To my step-daughter, Alisha. She has been a part of my life for over fourteen years and has become a beautiful young lady. I am very proud of her.

Most of all to my husband, Bob—my best friend. His love and support keep me going every day.

Remember if you trust in God, all things are possible. May all that you dream come true.

With all my love,
Linda

Contents

Hello

I haven't felt this way in years!
My heart feels light.
I am full of energy.
I have smiled all day.
You have touched my soul.
I have found myself almost dancing.
I feel almost . . . silly.
I feel wonderful!
I want this feeling to last forever!
It all started when you said
Hello.

The First Time

I've known since the very beginning,
that I was in love with you.
I looked into your eyes and I knew.
I knew right then and there.
It was so hard to breathe!
My heart beat wildly when you looked at me.
I couldn't concentrate.
You affected my whole life.
I couldn't eat.
I couldn't sleep.
I only thought about you.
About us.
When I looked into your eyes,
I knew that I loved you unconditionally.
I loved you with all of my soul!
With all that I am.
With all that I will ever be.

The Day Will Come

The day will come when you know that I am your friend.
I would never betray your trust.
I will always be there for you.
Time will not separate our friendship.
The day will come when you realize your secrets are safe with me.

I hope by now you already know this.
It's just so hard for you to trust people.
Your feelings have been locked tight for so many years.
They seem foreign . . . even to you.
I do understand, and I will wait.
The day will come when you realize that I like the real you.
It is easy to be your friend, just the way you are.
I don't want you to change.
I just want to be your friend.
I enjoy the times when we are together.
The day will come when you are confident with our friendship.
When you reach out, I will be there.
As you unlock the doors, it won't change how I feel about you.
If you would only realize how much you have to give people.
You are so special . . . so unique.
The day will come and I will be there.
I will always be your friend.

How Do I Find the Words?

When we are together, I don't know what to say.
My heart says how I feel.
How do I begin to tell you?
We joke, we laugh, and have long talks.
We avoid saying how we feel.
I love you more than I ever thought possible.
When we are apart, I feel so alone.
You are in all of my thoughts and dreams.
Someday I hope to tell you how I feel.
But for now, we will go on as we are.
I love you, and I need you.
I want these feelings to go on forever.
Can me make these dreams come true?
I want to find the courage to tell you how I feel.
When we are together, I don't know what to say.

Thoughts

When I am alone, I think of you.
I rehearse things that I'd say to you.
I invent conversations that we'd have.
I dream of your replies.

From these conversations I imagine peace.
A peace that I cannot find now.
A peace found in an honest relationship.

Sometimes when I am alone,
Thoughts of these conversations devour me.
They become so real,
I force myself to remember,
These conversations exist only in my mind.
They belong to me.

When you are here, or when you call,
My tongue is tied, and the words are locked in my heart.
My feelings for you are so intense they devour me.
I am acutely aware of my surroundings.
My thoughts become jumbled into a confused knot.
I rehearse the conversation in my mind once again.
Looking for the courage to tell you how I feel.

You said my head is always someplace else.
But you couldn't be further from the truth.
I am right here with you.
I am just searching for the key to unlock my heart.
My thoughts are always with you.

Do You Remember That Day?

I'll never forget your eyes.
You looked at me and read my heart.
You made me smile and laugh,
Like never before, and never since.

My heart was free for the day.
My troubles were forgotten.
Do you remember that day?

You were so relaxed and carefree.
You stopped playing silly word games,
I saw the real you.
The clouds and masks, had gone away,
I feel in love with you.

We walked, and we talked,
And we drove for miles. I will never forget you.
I wish I knew, if you felt it too.
Do you remember that day?

Confusion

I think about you day and night.
No one has ever confused me the way you do.
I try to understand what you do,
Who you are.
But after all this time,
You can still hurt me,
Without saying a word.
We can sit next to each other,
And talk for hours.

I want to know everything about you.
I'd like to understand who you really are.
Do you want any of these things?
I am so confused!
I do not understand you.
I want to, but I just don't.

It's so difficult sometimes.
Why can't we just stop playing
These childish games?
No one has ever confused me,
The way you do!

I Just Wanted You

Sitting here with a group of your friends,
I feel like an outcast.
I don't feel a part of the conversation.
I am cut off when I speak.
I am invisible.
I don't know the secret password.
I am not a part of your group.

No matter what I feel for you,
I'll never fit in.
I am so different from you and your friends.
I feel like they are dissecting me.
I can hear them talking about me,
As I leave the room.
I have been prejudged, tried, and hung!
They don't even know me.

I wanted you.
I didn't want to join a club.
I just wanted you.

Must I Always Find You?

You never ask me any questions.
You always accept whatever I tell you.
Never asking for more.
Never judging what I say.
You just accept me for what I am.

There have been times when acceptance,
Has meant so much.
But right now what I really want,
Is for you to ask me how I am.
I would really love an honest talk.
I would give anything to tell you
How I really feel.
And yet I wonder . . .
What would you really say?
Would the words you speak be out of
Love, obligation, or confusion?

All I want is for you to love me.
To even hear you say you care,
Would make my heart soar.
Will you ever seek me out?
Or must I always find you?

You Were the Only One

I started to tell you everything.
It was hard to get up the nerve.
I thought that I'd start at the beginning.
I never got that far.
I hesitated when the words were hard to say.
Then . . . WHAM!
You said something that changed the subject.

I wanted to talk to you.
It was my final attempt to trust you . . . with me.
I never even made it to the beginning.
You were the only one I thought would listen.
I thought you'd understand.
You were the only one.
Now I'll keep it all inside again.
I really had hoped that you could help me.

If you won't listen,
Then no one else will.
You were my last chance.
You were my last hope.
You were the only one.

Silence

I must have practiced in my head
what I'd say a thousand times.
You have no idea how long it took me
to say the things I did.

I was prepared for rejection.
I was prepared for acceptance.
I was not prepared for silence.

It's been days . . .
only silence.
It's turned into weeks . . .
only silence.
That hurts more than rejection.

Why Do You Always Leave?

I feel so safe in your arms.
The problems of the day,
All disappear.
I feel so close to you,
Like we're connected.
Your world is so very different than mine.
Your goals are so far away from my dreams.
How could we make this work?

I look into your eyes,
I feel your arms around me.
I feel so secure.
I want this feeling to last forever.
But as usual,
You leave.
I am left to figure out why.
Why do you always leave?

Equal Passion

I've never known anyone like you.
I can love you with all of my heart,
And the next minute . . .
I can be angry with you,
Just as passionately.
Passion is the perfect description.
I love you!
I'm angry with you!
Both with equal passion.
My feelings are so intense . . .
I get confused.

Someone Else

When you told me,
That you were in love with someone else,
My world stood still.
After searching for the courage,
I told you all that was locked in my heart.
You never said anything,
Only silence.
It was like I had never spoken to you.
It was not what I expected.

Do you realize how hard it was for me,
To say the things I said?
I had just poured out my soul to you,
I felt bare, exposed,
Your silence made my heart raw.

Finally after an eternity of waiting.
You said that you THINK that MAYBE you MIGHT
be in love with someone else.
You THINK!
MAYBE!
You MIGHT!
My world stood still.
My reply was as yours was,
SILENCE . . . only silence.

Waiting For You

I have forgotten what it was like,
To sit here and wait for you.
I can't seem to sleep in this empty bed.
You've been gone so much.

Each time I hear the door slam,
I hold my breath.
Waiting to hear your key in the lock.
I'm sure I'd never hear the key,
Over the loud pounding of my heart.

I have forgotten what it was like,
To sit here and wait for you.
There's a light in the window,
As a car draws nearer.
My heart is pounding wildly.
I take a deep breath . . . and . . .
Sigh . . . as the car drives by.

When will you come home?
Are you alone?
I have forgotten how painful it is,
Sitting here and waiting for you!

I Wish You Would Just Come Home

The thunder roars, and I'm afraid!
I sit here all alone.
I try to be strong, I try to be brave,
I wish you'd just come home!

The sky sounds so angry,
Almost as angry as you,
I'm confused by your anger,
And bothered it by it too.
I don't seem to make you happy,
No matter what I do.

I don't feel that I belong here,
I don't seem to fit in there.
The sky is turning an ominous hue.
I am lonely and afraid,
What do I do?

I hope the sun will shine tomorrow,
Maybe it will shed some light.
We're in this together, I need the strength to fight.

The thunder roars, and I'm afraid!
I try to be strong, I try to be brave.
I sit here all alone.
I just wish you'd come home!

How Do You Feel?

I don't even know who you are anymore.
I don't know how I feel.
I know that I love you.
There is a new tone in your voice.
One that I don't understand.
I don't know you anymore.
I don't know what your dreams are.
What are your goals?
Do you know what mine are?
Do you know what I want from life?
What do you see when you look at me?
Will we grow old together?
Will you look at me with love then?
Or will you simply look around me,
As you do now.

You Have Broken My Heart

There is an emptiness deep inside of me.
I feel completely lost.
You broke my heart on purpose.
You walked all over my feelings.
Then you smile as if nothing happened.
You act so innocent of my pain.
You must have some idea of what you've done.
How could you be so cold?
You never say how you feel anymore.
You know what my feelings are.
You purposely did this to hurt me.
Why are you breaking my heart?
What have I done to deserve this?
I haven't taken anything from you.
I haven't asked you for anything.
I would never purposely try to hurt you.
My feelings cannot be turned off and on.
My heart doesn't have a switch.
Am I supposed to just stop loving you?
I'll never forget you.
I'll always love you.
You have broken my heart!

I Must Be Different

It's finally clear to me.
Why did it take so long?
I'm really a fool.
What I wanted,
And what I needed,
Clouded what really was.

You understood me.
You knew how I felt.
You knew what you said
Would hurt me!

I have spent a lot of time thinking
About what was,
And what could have been.
It's all I have!
What I am now,
Is nothing.
I have no goals for the future.

If you think I will gain perspective
Through your painful words
It won't work!
All it does is hurt me.
I've been hurt so much.
I guess I should apologize,
For how deeply I feel things.
No one has ever understood.
It must be me.
I must be different.

I'm Sorry

To simply
say that
I AM SORRY
does not
seem to
be enough.
But it
is all
that I
have.

Is all
enough?

My Place

Once again you've put me in my place,
Whatever that is.
You get my hopes up,
My dreams become reality.
A fantasy comes true.
Every move that I make,
Is in anticipation of you.

Once again you've put me in my place,
Whatever that is.

Our next conversation I find you almost cold.
Your voice is merely tolerant,
And I am sorry that I called.

Once again you've put me in my place,
Whatever that is.

My hopes, my dreams, my fantasies
They are all connected to you.
If you'd only clear the air,
Then I'd know what to expect.

Once again you've put me in my place,
Whatever that is.

Goodbye My Friend

You have always been my dream.
My fantasy.
When things go wrong,
I always find myself thinking of you.
When I am alone,
I think about things that we've done.
Times that we've shared.
What am I going to do now?
How do I get through the tough times?
You have always been my rock, my support.
Now that you have gone from my dreams,
I feel empty.
I miss you.
I will always miss the feelings,
that you evoke in me.
Goodbye my friend.

Just Not Me

Just when I think I can let go,
You change my mind.
Just when I think I can make it on my own,
You remind me just how weak I am.
Just when I'm sure that,
You can't hurt me anymore,
You show me that you can.
Just when I really need you,
You're gone.
Were you ever really there?
Or did I just want you to be there.
You have never needed me.
You say that you don't need anyone.
Maybe you'll need someone,
Just not me.

I Just Never Could Forget

Forgive and forget

Words that are easy to say,
They are very hard for me to do.
I forgave you a long time ago.
We don't talk about it.
Yet I just can't forget.

Sometimes I wonder if you remember it too.
What do you remember about those times?
I remember Pain . . . intense pain!
A wild blinding fear that knew no end.
A panic so intense, I could not compare.

My life changed after that.
I've never been the same.
I keep trying to be, What you want me to be.
I've completely lost myself.
I've lost who I am.
I just never could forget.

Goodbye

I have to say goodbye.
I know that the time has come.
In my heart I know that it's right.
I guess I've always known,
It would come to this.
But now that the time is here,
I'm afraid.
I have to say goodbye.

I just sit here and cry.
I knew in my heart that it would end.
There's too many fences,
That we'd need to mend.
Where do I put all of these feelings?
So many things I've never said.
How do I lay all of this to rest?
I have to say goodbye.

You'll never know,
Just how much I've cried.
You'll never know,
I'll never say.
It's just over,
It has to be this way.
Goodbye.

US

It has just occurred to me.
When I think of you,
I automatically think of US.
That's funny . . .
Or maybe a better word would be sad.

There is no US.
There never has been.
Only you.
Only me.
Very separate. To think of all the lost time.
Time that I'll never get back.
For years now,
I've thought in terms of US.

I feel very alone.
So very alone!
There is no US!
Only you.
Only me.

The Little Things

Do you sometimes think,
of how things used to be?
I DO.
Sometimes late at night,
when I can't fall asleep,
I remember all the little things.
Your face, your smile, something you said,
the way you looked here or there.
Sometimes even certain smells,
will bring back memories of the past.
It can be so real!
It's almost like it just happened.

Sometimes I hear an old song,
that reminds me of you.
Even some new songs make me stop and listen.
And I wonder . . .
When you hear that song, do you think of me?
Do you remember all the little things?
I DO.
I wonder if you know,
Just how often,
I think about you.

I Miss You

I woke up this morning,
And I thought of you.
I saw people all day,
That reminded me of you.
I spent the whole evening,
With you on my mind.
I went to bed, And you filled my dreams.
You fill my whole day,
Yet we never see each other.
You are my best and closest friend,
But at times I don't know you.
We can tell each other anything,
And never use words.
We are miles apart,
Yet, I am still with you.
I am here.
You are there.
How much longer will we be apart?
When will we be together?
I MISS YOU!

The Lonely Sunset

Sitting here on the beach,
looking across the water.
There's no relief from the heat,
In fact I think it's getting hotter.
The sea gulls fly across the sky,
If you listen, you'll hear them cry.
The water continually races toward the shore.
My thoughts return to you once more.

How I wish that you were here with me.
What a beautiful sunset we would see.
I sit here and watch the sunset all alone.
Then I slowly walk down the path toward home.
The dark, gloomy trees softly whisper,
The noises that I hear make me walk swifter.
I breathe a sigh of relief when I reach the door.
My thoughts race again to you once more.

In the distance . . .
The water still races toward the shore.
The sea gulls cry,
And the trees whisper your name.
Just like before.

It was another lonely sunset.

I Am Lonely

I love you! I want you!
Sometimes
I need you.

Being with you,
Is something
I long for
each day.

Why did you
Move so far
Away?

I
AM
LONELY!

Tick-Tick

Night after night I go to bed alone.
I wake up frightened,
And there's no one there.
There's no one to tell me
Things will be alright.
No one to hold me
So that I can sleep.
I go to bed alone.
I wake up alone.

My days are filled with survival
Until dark.
My nights are filled with anticipation,
Of the sunrise.
I live each day without passion.
I live routinely.
My life is on autopilot.
I am alone and frightened.
There is no one to tell.

The clock ticks loudly in the other room.
TICK-TICK
My thoughts flow in rhythm to its beat.
TICK-TICK
Alone.
TICK-TICK
Alone.

Housewife Blues

I need to have someone come home to me at night.
Someone who will share things with me.
Someone who can take the pain
Out of this loneliness I feel.
Someone to hold me at night.

Everything has piled up on me
These past few years.
I'M TIRED!
I'm tired of being alone.
I need to share my life with someone!

I love my children more than anything!
But sometimes I need another adult to talk to.
I don't like to be alone.
For days and days,
It's just the kids and I.

I am losing my identity.
I've lost who I wanted to be!
I merely exist.
I do the same old thing.
The same old way.
Day in and day out.
Something has to change.

Glue

I feel pulled in so many directions.
For the past several years I merely exist.
I chauffeur people places,
I cook, I clean, I take care of the sick,
Even when I am sick myself.
I do the laundry.
I hold things together when you're gone.
I'M GLUE.

I hold things together.
I am caught in the middle.
I take care of everyone's needs but my own.
It's been so long,
I don't even know what my needs are.
I'M GLUE!

Runny, sticky, drippy, drying clear.
It holds things together.
That's me! I'M GLUE!

Clear . . . invisible.
No one notices the glue,
Only what it's holding together.
I'M GLUE!

Switching Gears

It's hard to switch gears at the end of the day.
I race all day long, doing this, and doing that.
I pick up this and drop off that.
The kids go here and there
Then comes the magic hour of nine o-clock.
The kids are in bed.
It's time to slow down.
The dishes need to be done.
The laundry needs to be put away.
OH YEA . . .

There's the project that the kids need to take
To school tomorrow.
The one they mentioned when I tucked them in.
Meanwhile, it's gotten late.
It's already time to go to bed.
I lie here in bed thinking,
Of all the things I need to do tomorrow.
I put the same thing on the top of my list,
That has been there for several years now.
1. Take time off for myself today.
That's usually the only thing left,
On my list to do each day.
It's the only thing that never gets a check mark.
It's hard switching gears.

If Only

I want you to believe in me.
If you believe in me,
Then maybe I can believe in myself.
If I can believe in myself,
Then maybe I could be someone.
I want to be someone!
If only you would believe in me.

Questions

What do you think of when you look at me?
Do you say to yourself,
"How could she let this happen?"
or
"Why doesn't she go on a diet?"
or
"Maybe if she'd just cut back on her eating?"
or
"Why doesn't she do something?"

What do you see when you look at me?
Do you look around me?
Do you try to avoid looking at me?
Do you just pretend not to notice my weight?

I'll tell you what's inside of me.
I'm ashamed, guilty, and embarrassed.
I feel like a failure, unworthy of love.
I'm humiliated at the pity I see in your eyes.
The harder I try, the more I fail.
I'm always in pain.
Both physical and mental.
I cover it up each day with a smile.
That way no one notices when I hurt.
It hurts when you can no longer look me in the eyes.

I Am Nobody

How does someone become a nobody?
How do you go from being someone with meaning,
To a nobody?

I once had direction and purpose,
A real meaningful life.
How did I become lost?

I have what I thought I wanted.
But now my life is without meaning.
I exist from day to day.
I have no dreams, no goals.
I am merely here.
I want to make a difference.
I just don't know how yet.
Today I am a nobody.
But when we meet tomorrow,
I will be someone! I will make a difference!
I will matter!

Diets! Diets! Diets!

I am drowning.
I am swallowed up by confusion.
I don't like how I feel.
I don't like how I look.
I want to help myself.
I want to be thinner.

I remember what it was like,
to be thin.
I want to feel that way again.

It's on the radio, it's in the mail,
Every magazine, every T.V. commercial,
FOOD—DIETS, FOOD—DIETS
If I wasn't constantly reminded,
Of what I cannot have,
Maybe, just maybe, I could succeed.
Maybe for once I'd have control.
I might even like myself.

DIETS—DIETS—DIETS
In my dictionary it means failure!

Who Am I?

When I stop and look into the mirror,
I become frightened.
Who am I?
What has happened to me?
How did I become this person?
I don't even recognize myself!
Who is this person looking back at me?
Where is the smile?
Where is the backbone?
Where is the confidence?
How did I become this pathetic creature?
How could I not see what was happening to me?
How did I loose control?
How could I be so blind?
How?
Where? When did this happen?
Who am I?

The Unwanted Doll

If you were to see me from the inside out.
You would see this frightened little girl.
I'd be huddled in the corner.
Needing someone to accept me.
Longing for attention.
Desperately wanting to be loved.

If you were to walk by this little girl,
You'd see a child broken,
Like an old doll.
A doll that no one wanted.
A doll that someone tossed into the garage,
Because it was beyond repair.
You'd see the real me.

The lonelier I get,
The heavier I get.
The heavier I get,
The more I bury that little girl.
The more I bury that little girl,
The less that anyone looks at me.
I am hiding beyond my weight.

What Do You See When You Look At Me?

So much of my life has changed.
I have made so many mistakes.
I wish I could control my jealousy.
I am suspicious of everything.
I keep remembering my past.
I will never forget the intense pain I felt.
It was suffocating!

I was to spend the rest of my life with you.
Can you live with my mistrust and doubt?
I hate what I've become.

What do you see when you look at me?
What do you feel when we touch?
What will we do when we grow old?
What will you think of me then? Will you love me?
Will you leave me?
Will you touch me?
Will you know me?
Will you know what's in my heart?
Or will we exist.
Separately.
Never knowing,
Never talking,
Always wondering,
Never knowing why.
What do you see when you look at me?

Care Enough to Look Inside

Once again I was able to pass by another mirror.
I can no longer look at myself.
When I do my hair, I only look at my hair.
I match my clothes on my bed.
When I'm dressed, I don't do a final check
to see if all is right.
I don't look in mirrors.
I stopped wearing makeup.
It's less time I spend in front of a mirror.
I can avoid mirrors forever.

If you truly love me,
Please help me.
Care enough to look inside me.
I am still there.
I just need your help to get out.
It's a very hard struggle!
I've been there before.

Please know that I try.
I try each and every day for a new beginning.
I feel my failure more than you can ever imagine.
So please . . . PLEASE . . .
Care enough to look inside.

A Life

To live is to dream.
To have a dream, is to live.
To have a goal,
Is to have a purpose.
To live and to dream,
Is the purpose of the goal.
To have none of this,
Is to be nothing.
In order to be nothing,
You have to want nothing.
To want nothing,
Prevents growing.
Not to grow,
Would be a shame.
And that would be a waste of life.
Everyone deserves a life.

Waiting

I watched you all in green,
As they rolled you down the hall.
Everything was so white,
so clean, so sterilized.
There were strangers all around you,
and I who loved you,
had to just sit here and wait.

They rolled you through the double doors,
their closing sounded so final.
Now all that I can do,
is just sit here and wait.

I looked at the clock on the wall.
Was it broken?
I checked my watch again,
I even tapped it a few times,
just to see that it wasn't broken.

Time moves so slowly,
when all you can do,
is just sit and wait.
I keep thinking of all the things,
I forgot to tell you.

I Pray, I Cry, I Pray

As I sit here in the chapel,
it is so quiet.
Somewhere in the distance,
I hear a clock ticking.
Why am I the only one here?
Am I the only one waiting for news?
I pray, I cry, I pray.

I don't understand.
I know there is a reason for this to happen.
I have to trust and pray.
Why am I the only one here?
The waiting rooms are full.
Why am I the only one here?
I pry, I cry, I pray.

Ninety-Five Steps to the Coffee Machine

I tell myself . . . Think of something else!
Don't concentrate on the waiting.
I tell myself . . . Try to forget how afraid you are.
I HATE WAITING!

Fifty-nine paces to the elevator.
Fourteen steps to the drinking fountain.
Ninety-five steps to the coffee machine.
Sixty-three paces to the nurses station.
Thirty-two paces to the rest room.

Here I find myself taking paper towels,
To wipe up the water spills.
I'm cleaning the counter!
I hear a doctor being paged.
I HATE WAITING!

Thirty-two steps to the waiting room.
A lady is watching a T.V. soap.
Another is doing needlepoint.
There is a group in the corner,
Huddled together crying.
Don't look at them!
I silently scream to myself.
THAT—WILL—NOT—BE—ME!
Everything will be alright.
It has to be.
I need to move.
Ninety-five steps to the coffee machine.

Fingerprints

Our minds are like windows.
We can look out and see life.
If in our lonely hours,
We lean upon our window,
We will smudge it with fingerprints.
When we lean upon the window,
Too often, or for too long,
Our vision becomes cloudy.
Everything gets confused.
You can't see clearly.
The fingerprints will cloud your mind.
Eventually our window becomes a door.
Only you can clean your windows.

What's In a Rainbow?

A rainbow holds the key
To love, understanding,
Companionship, happiness,
Life, and yourself.
For those who seek life,
And are not greedy,
They shall find the answers,
At the end of time.
For those who only seek
The pot of gold at the end,
They will never truly find out,
What life was truly about.

Magical Snow

As the snow falls, it glistens like tiny diamonds
falling from the sky. Each shimmers and glows,
with a brilliance that can be compared to nothing known.

The tiny sparkling flakes dance their way to the ground.
First one, then another; soon the ground is covered with
a glow that's almost blinding. Night becomes almost daylight
under the moon. For as far as the eye can see,
there is a fresh innocence to the land.

Looking across the snow-covered hills, it covers so much
of the hate and anger out there. Don't rush the moment away,
for all too soon the magic will be gone. Things will change
very quickly. Soon things will be ugly and dirty.
 There will be tracks and trails. Life will go on, and the magic will be gone.

This moment will be gone forever.

Too Hot to Sleep

It is so warm tonight. There is a faint breeze, blowing the curtains. In the distance, I can hear the water lapping at the shoreline. The night is quiet and still. Somewhere down the beach, a baby cries. As I look into the darkness, I see a fire down on the shoreline. Surrounding the fire appears to be a family. Someone paces back and forth. Over and over again, like a panther trapped in a cage. Slowly the crying tops, and the shadowy figure stops pacing. The movement becomes a continuous gentle rocking from side to side. All is quiet, and the air is still. I breathe in slow, shallow breaths, so as not to disturb the stillness of the night. A streak of lightning flashes across the distant sky. Its reflection on the water is startling. Hours later the beach is empty. The clouds roll in with furious intensity. As the clouds open, the rain begins to fall. Its soft patter, through the leaves on the trees, gently floats to the fern-covered ground. There is a steady rhythm as the rain falls and the wind blows. The water rushes toward the shore. The stillness is gone, and at last I can fall asleep.

The Old Lighthouse

As I drive down the dusty, dirty road, the anticipation builds as I return to a place that I haven't been since I was a child. I remember the lighthouse. It was as bright as the sun. It was sitting on a point, with its red flashing light to warn the boat of pending danger. The beach around the lighthouse was like night and day. The waves were high on one side. They would come crashing down with such avenging force. The other side was always calm. The water there was quiet and playful. Everyone lined this shore with abundance. People would walk barefoot in the sand and play games in the water. The children would build sand castles or play on the swings at the park near the beach. On the other side, only a few people could be found. There the shoreline was full of stones, and the water grew deep very quickly. I remembered The soft, low moan of the lighthouse horn. I could hardly wait to see it all again! I was almost there! I noticed up ahead that the road was blocked. There was a sign that said "ROAD CLOSED." How could this be? I parked the car and began to walk down the winding road. As I rounded the corner, I was completely taken by surprise. The lighthouse had boards over the windows, and the paint was cracked and peeling. The soft, low moan seemed like a cry for help. The beach was closed, and the swings were in the water. The angry side had crashed through and swallowed up the calm side. All that is left of the place I once loved are my memories.

Sunset

The wind softly whispers in the trees. You can hear the leaves rustle. The twigs snap as a little squirrel races off to hide its new-found treasure. I sit there quietly watching, never moving, barely daring to breathe. I'm afraid to move for fear the squirrel will drops its precious treasure and run. The puffy clouds in the sky are turning into cotton candy shades. The sun is slowly beginning to fall into the water. The clouds go from pink to orange, then to reds and purples. The water races toward the shore, reaching, grabbing gently, and then returning to the dark depths from where it came. I begin to breathe to the rhythm of the water's soft sounds. The sun is slipping lower, and it leaves a golden path across the water. The magical path sparkles and shimmers as the sun slowly begins to touch the waves. If you sit very still, and you are very quiet, you can almost see the magic. The sun slips into the water, and you can almost see the steam rise. Ssssshhhhhhh . . . the water puts out the sun's fiery heat. The sky remains orange and purple. The crickets and the frogs serenade me as darkness creeps in. The wind softly whispers in the trees.

Errata

The following are corrections for typographical errors in the text.

P. 4, line 13: "can me make these" should read "can we make these."

P. 41, line 8: "I was to spend" should read "I want to spend."

P. 45, line 14: "I pry, I cry" should read "I pray, I cry."

P. 51, line 4: "to warn the boat" should read "to warn the boats."